How

Worrying and

Start Living

- What Other People Think Of Me Is None Of My Business

Learn Stress Management and How To Overcome Relationship Jealousy, Social Anxiety and Stop Being Insecure

Introduction

Stress is a lot like love – hard to define, but you know it when you feel it.

This book will explore the nature of stress and how it infiltrates every level of your life, including the physical, emotional, cognitive, relational and even spiritual. You'll find ways to nurture resilience, rationality and relaxation in your every day life, and learn how to loosen the grip of worry and anxiety. Through techniques that get to the heart of your unique stress response, and an exploration of how stress can affect your relationships, you'll discover how to control stress instead of letting it control you. This book shows you how.

Chapter 1: Why You Should Read This Book

You wake up in the morning, swatting at the snooze button and cursing the start of a new day. You're utterly exhausted, already. Maybe you fight to get the kids up, get dressed, and start the daily errands. Work grinds on you, and your partner feels like he or she is drifting away from you as your connection wavers under endless niggles and arguments about money and housework. Everything you encounter irritates and exasperates you.

It seems like every day goes like this. You race from one thing to the next, wiped out at the end of it all and seemingly never done with everything you have to do. By the early afternoon, your brain is in a grey fog and you're snapping at everyone. You can't remember a time when you didn't feel cynical and bitter about life.

At night you collapse into bed, knowing that the following day, the same cycle will only start again. Maybe you lie there and worry about getting old or sick or dying, or worry that your life is slipping past you, or about your children or your marriage. Have you had your vitamins today? Paid the credit card? Fixed the leak in the sink? Fed the dog? Gone to gym? Called your mother? Sometimes, you're not even sure what you're anxious about. You only know that the world seems hostile, life seems hard and most of the time you simply feel overwhelmed.

Does this sound like you?

Stress has become so commonplace in our modern world that we are actually suspicious of people who claim not to be busy. Our lives keep filling up with more: more events, more responsibilities, more things, more people, more work. Like a bewildered rat in its wheel, we decide there's only one thing to do: *keep going*.

The consequences may not be obvious immediately, but the effects of stress, anxiety and worry are far-reaching. Wear and tear from stress can include heart disease, increased risk of cancer and even early death. Stress makes you feel awful, obviously, but it's far more serious than that. A stressed out body and mind are simply not everything they could be. Being overwhelmed cognitively means you are never really 100% available to make the best decisions for yourself. You're slower, get tired more quickly, and your memory suffers.

When you're constantly juggling feelings of stress, you're not *emotionally* available either. You're more prone to depression and pessimism, more likely to abandon projects you start and more likely to interpret things around you in a negative light. Stress also seeps into your relationships. The last thing you want to do is seek out others and be social, and this together with an irritable mood and short temper mean your closest connections become undermined.

You don't necessarily have to be a rushed-off-her-feet working mother or a CEO who's married to his high pressure job to understand how damaging stress can be to your relationships. For those of us with social anxiety, shyness or difficulties with dating, relationships with others are actually the *cause* of the stress. Low self esteem, paranoia about the judgment of others, inability to reach out to the opposite sex... Even when you manage to find someone, jealousy and insecurity sabotage your ability to relax and enjoy it. These are all just different manifestations of this strange frame of mind we call "stress".

Stress gets into your body, heart, mind and soul. Stress damages your ability to have trusting, open relationships with others. Saddest of all, stress weakens your relationship with yourself in the form of self doubt, low self confidence and bitterness. We tend to think of stress as nothing more serious than a certain tightness in the shoulders or a schedule that could be a little leaner. But stress can permeate every single area of our lives, right from the presence of stress hormones in the body's tissues to our bigger, overarching sense of who we are as human beings in this world. This book is for those of us pacing in our cages, tossing at night with heads full of doom and gloom, unable to trust those around us and the world at large. Here is a list of the ways that stress might manifest in different areas of life. If any of the following apply to you, this book was written for you.

Symptoms of Stress – The 5 Levels

Physical symptoms:

* Frequently having accidents, being clumsy and rushing
* Neck, shoulder and back tension. Muscle spasms and tension headaches
* Diarrhea or constipation, ulcers, indigestion or heartburn
* Increase or decrease in appetite; cravings for stimulants like caffeine
* Disturbed sleep, including nightmares, insomnia or oversleeping
* Changes in weight; weight gain particularly around the waist
* Low energy levels
* Acne, teeth grinding, dry skin, brittle nails, frequent

infections

* Seeking out substances, addiction and self medication

Emotional symptoms:

* Feeling overwhelmed
* Feeling sad, or like you have no hope and might as well give up
* No longer being interested in what used to excite you
* Being irritable and having a short temper
* Feeling apathetic and indifferent
* Feeling guilty and worthless
* Feeling mistrustful and suspicious of others' motivations
* Tearfulness and sensitivity to criticism

Cognitive and behavioral symptoms:

* Absentmindedness
* Procrastination and avoidance
* Being unable to properly concentrate
* Distractibility
* Feeling unorganized and unfocused, not completing projects
* Constantly negative thoughts

Relational symptoms:

* Feeling like everyone wants a piece of you
* Cynicism about relationships or family
* Loss of libido
* Low self esteem
* Shallow connections with others
* Feeling antisocial; withdrawing socially

Spiritual symptoms:

* Feeling alone in the world
* Feeling unable to summon any hope or optimism
* A crisis of faith
* A sense of purposelessness
* Feeling disconnected from others
* Feeling that life has no meaning or is chaotic

The above list is by no means exhaustive. The way stress manifests in our lives is as unique as we are and, as you can see, stress can show its face in many different ways, along any of these 5 levels. When we are in environments that are not supportive to us, when we lack the skills to adapt to challenges around us, or when we've simply expected more of ourselves than is humanly possible, we experience stress.

But this book is not just another "anti-stress" book. Here, we will not be concerned with only reducing the *symptoms* of stress. Rather, we'll try to understand exactly *what* stress is and the role it plays in our lives. We'll attempt to dig deep to really understand the real sources of our anxiety and how to take ownership of them. Using the power of habit and several techniques for smoothing out the stressful wrinkles in our day-to-day lives, we'll move towards a real-world solution to living with less stress, more confidence and a deep spiritual resilience that will insulate you from the inevitable pressures of life.

This book will be a little different from most stress-management tools on the market today. While most stress solutions offer relief for symptoms in only one or two of these areas, this book will show you how all 5 areas are important, and a successful stress solution will touch on each of them.

By adopting a trusting, open and relaxed attitude, we'll bring something more of ourselves to relationships of all kinds. This books will take a look at dating and relationships without stress and worry, as well as ways to bring tranquility and balance into your home and family life. Again, this book is not about eradicating stress from your life forever. We'll end with a consideration of the *positive* side of negative thinking, and how we can use stress and worry to our advantage.

Chapter 2: What Stress/Worry Really is

Stress is a complicated phenomenon. However, it's even more complicated than most people give it credit for. To put it simply, stress is primarily a physical response to the world around us. Almost every animal experiences stress of this kind. As creatures that needed to defend themselves and their families in sometimes hostile environments, human beings have also evolved to recognize danger and remove themselves from it as quickly as possible.

Stress, in this case, is a sudden and intense state of arousal that forces an action – running away, fighting or paying very close attention to an emergency situation. Stress is our bodies' natural way of telling us that something needs to change. We perceive a danger, and our bodies alert us to get out of that situation.

But, unless you have a particularly stressful work environment, dealing with lions and snakes and other deadly animals is simply no longer a part of daily life. Modern man has not had to deal with threats to his life to quite the same degree as his ancestors. For most people today, life is blissfully free of natural disasters, warring tribes, strange diseases and animal attacks.

Our innate stress response is older than our civilization, however, and is very much with us today. In the past, the human body perceived a threat and responded by producing hormones like cortisol and adrenaline. These hormones would make it easier for the human to "fight or flight". Stress was a useful mechanism that prepared the body to stand its ground and defend itself or else hightail it and get to safety.

Anyone with High School biology will know this. But in today's world, the things that stress us are subtler, more persistent, and more psychological than a bear lurking in the bushes. These days, our bodies react to other perceived threats – the loss of a job or a spouse, for example. While these things don't directly threaten our survival, we have come to *perceive* them as if they do. Even though we don't need to run away or fight with our bare hands anymore, *our physical response is still the same*: our bodies flood with stress hormones. Understanding this evolutionary predisposition to stress helps us understand how to deal with it. Biologically, stress evolved as a physical response to the world around us. But this helpful adaptation is sometimes... not so helpful. What may have served our ancient ancestors can be more of a hindrance to us today. Consider the example of Mike:

Mike is walking down a dark alleyway at night. He hears brisk footsteps behind him. The area is known for its crime. His pulse picks up, he becomes very alert, and he stops thinking of anything else. His entire mind and body become tuned into this possible threat. He turns around and sees a stranger in the shadows who appears to be holding something in his hand. He has the thought, " I may be in danger", which is putting it pretty accurately.

He's keenly aware that if he wants to make it out of this threatening situation, he'd better use whatever he can. He scans around, looking for other people, and speeds up his pace. Where's the nearest police station? He tries to think if he has anything on him that could be used as a weapon. His heart is throbbing in his ears – if he needs to run, he'll do it. *As fast as he can.*

The footsteps continue gaining on him. He's almost running when he finally gets to a busy intersection and quickly catches a cab to get out of there as fast as he can. He relaxes a little. The adrenaline slowly drains away and he stops shaking. He even cracks a smile – he's alive! He's safe now, and gradually allows other thoughts to enter his mind again. He thinks, "That was close, but it's over now" and he's right. He berates himself for being in such an alleyway this late at night in the first place. After 10 minutes, it's as if nothing happened.

Picture another scenario. Mike arrives home after his little ordeal in the alleyway. Instead of his wife meeting him at the door as she usually does, he sees her chatting and laughing on the phone with someone. When she sees him, she quickly ends the call and comes over to say hello. There's something different about her, but he can't say what. He has the thought, "I bet she's cheating on me."

It's a thought he won't admit to, a thought he's embarrassed to have, but it makes him angry nevertheless. As he sits down for a drink and watches some TV, his heart is racing, and he has trouble thinking of anything else. Just as he did earlier that evening, he has the unconscious feeling, "I am in danger". He has an imaginary argument with her in his mind, and doesn't notice his jaw clenching and his muscles tightening. He remembers all the other "evidence" he has to support his suspicion. The thought of his wife leaving him would tear his world apart – what would he do without her? How dare she? Does she think he's an idiot? How could she do that to him? Slowly, the thoughts pump him full of adrenaline and cortisol.

Both of these situations could be described as "stressful". But unlike the alley situation, when there was clearly a point at which the danger was gone, he has no clear way to know whether this threat of his wife's infidelity is gone or not. So he never breathes a sigh of relief and thinks, "That was a close call, but it's over now." While the first wave of stress was over as soon as the threat was, the situation with his wife is a little more complicated.

He goes to bed, the stress hormones still coursing through him, the thoughts still firmly lodged in his mind. In fact, he could live years of his life like this, a constant low grade sense of threat underscoring everything. In the same way that he couldn't think of much else when he was preoccupied with his survival in the dark alley way, he couldn't reasonably think properly when his mind was trying to process the perceived threat of his wife's cheating. Cognitively, he can't rest. He *looks* just fine, but biochemically, cognitively, even spiritually, he is a being who is laboring under a very real threat. He is safe and comfortable in his middle class house, yet at a molecular level, he resembles nothing more than a caveman running for his life. It's no wonder that people who carry such burdens end up driving themselves to early heart attacks.

The mechanisms we have evolved to deal with stress are a little primitive, but they work in situations of obvious, physical danger. Modern man, however, is a social creature and not nearly as beholden to natural laws as he was before. To put it simply, we have not evolved subtle enough ways to deal with the new "dangers" we encounter every day. What good is fight or flight when we deal with people spreading gossip about us?

Or when we worry about our life choices as we lay in bed at night? Mike's teeth grinding and muscle tensing do nothing to help him out of his sticky situation with his wife.

It is not simply enough to let out bodies take care of our stress response. To cope with the demands of our culturally complex society, we need a more deliberate and more conscious way of dealing with stress. In fact, it is often our inbuilt biological mechanisms that betray us the most: the responses we have evolved over millennia are simply no match for the social landscape we find ourselves in.

The way we process stress may start out in the biological realm, but it quickly becomes more complex than that. Our physical stress response radiates out into the realm of the emotional and the cognitive, poisoning our ability to connect with others and, at the broadest level, even altering our spiritual being.

The difference between us and ancient man is that we possess a heightened consciousness and the ability to make choices about how we behave. We can become aware of our thoughts and habits, and in doing so, we can decide what thoughts to nurture and which to abandon. What follows is a conscious look at every level in which stress can have an effect.

We'll begin with a look at techniques to tame our fight or flight response, i.e. the *physical* symptoms of stress. Next, we'll explore how our thoughts can affect the way we experience stress, and look at ways to incorporate more healthful thoughts and habits into our daily life. Then, we'll look at how these thoughts are also interconnected with the way we interact emotionally with others, whether in dating or with our families. Lastly, we'll consider the bigger, spiritual picture of stress and try to construct our own personalized "stress map".

Chapter 3: The Physical Level: Relief From the Physical Symptoms of Stress

To begin, you might want to know of ways that can reliably reduce your feelings of stress and worry, *right now*. Sometimes, when insomnia feels like it's eating you alive, all you want is quick relief. Stress at this level looks like irritability, headaches and sore muscles. Here are some techniques that will help you soothe the first, physical level of stress that we all experience from time to time.

Progressive Muscle Relaxation:

People aren't entirely sure why, but it seems that muscles are able to go into a deeper state of relaxation when they try to relax after first tensing up a little. You can use this to your advantage with this simple method that relaxes each and every muscle and tissue in your body. Practiced once a day, progressive muscle relaxation can be a huge help for chronic pain, insomnia and general feelings of tension.

Find a quiet, comfortable place where you won't be disturbed for at least half an hour. You could also try this at bed time as you drift off to sleep. Lay down and let all your limbs hang loose. Close your eyes and take a few minutes to find your breath and slow it down, taking in fresh oxygen and slowly releasing it again.

Start at your feet and focus on the many muscles there. Become aware of them, and give each a good squeeze as you tense up the muscles in your toes or arch your feet. Really stretch and enjoy the intense feeling, holding for a few seconds.

Then, very, very slowly, let all of that tension go again. Feel your muscles loosening and expanding, and try to draw out the sensation of letting everything go. If you like, do the process again, or move onto the next body part. Travel up and tense/relax your legs, back muscles and arms. Take your time. Finish off with more deep breathing – if you're still awake, that is...

Guided imagery:

Start in much the same way as you did for the previous exercise, although you can also sit, if you prefer. Close your eyes and let your mind wander. Breathe deeply and slowly. Think of a place - any place. Choose a special place that can be, from now on, your "sanctuary". You may choose an isolated desert, a beautiful woodland forest or the top of a fantasy castle. It doesn't matter, it's your sanctuary, so make sure it's a place that really resonates with you.

Now take your time to explore and flesh out this world. Engage all your senses as you imagine every tiniest detail. How does it smell? Feel? What can you hear? What can you see? Picture it all, and linger on the details. This is crucial. When you have painted a full and rich picture of this sanctuary, go further inward and summon up a calm, happy emotion. Dwell on your feelings of peace and bliss, and link these feelings with the new place you've built for yourself. Tell your unconscious mind that you can come here whenever you are stressed and overwhelmed.

The next time you are feeling frazzled and irritable, take a few moments out of your day to pay a visit to your special place. Just close your eyes and devote the next few minutes to reminding yourself of all the lovely, tranquil things you found there before. No matter how busy or anxious you feel, rest in the knowledge that this place is always there, and accessible with just a few breaths.

Other stress relief tips:

- Take up yoga, tai chi, gardening, hiking or any other gentle physical exercise that gets you out of your head.

- Consider doing something creative or non verbal, such as sketching, pottery or even cooking.

- Get a pet – there are studies supporting the fact that they help reduce stress levels.

- Learn to delegate. If you have too little time to do everything you need to in a day, seriously consider if you should hire some extra help or assign tasks to family or co-workers.

- Look into meditation. This is another area with a lot of scientific studies to back it up. You can do this either alone or with a group, and try to build moments of mindfulness into your schedule. Many people find Zen Buddhist literature or other spiritual principles very grounding in their journey out of stressful living.

- Vow to give up multitasking.

- Watch your diet: processed foods, alcohol, caffeine, too little water, excess sugar or too much refined carbohydrate in your diet can disrupt your mood and make it more difficult to relax and unwind.

- Speak to your doctor about a natural or mild anxiety

medication – St. John's Wort has been shown in clinical trials to reduce feelings of anxiety.

- Exercise – another area with strong evidence behind it. The endorphins and sense of accomplishment are some of the best antidotes to stress.

- Give yourself breaks – and defend those breaks. So many people let work or obligations creep into their down time. Section off parts of your schedule where you don't work or fuss with other commitments. Don't let *anything* disturb that time.

Chapter 4: The Cognitive and Emotional Level: What You are (Really) Stressed About, or, How to Take a "Stress Reading"

Now that you have a few techniques for managing the physical side of your stress response, you can pay attention to the other levels. You may have found that no matter how much you relax your muscles, stressful thoughts can easily undo all your hard work and leave you tense and wound up again.

Imagine that stress is a kind of instrument that gives you readings about the way your body, mind and spirit are functioning. High stress, or a needle dangerously hovering into the red zone on your instrument, is not a problem in itself. It's only a *symptom* of a problem. Take sedatives, distract yourself or try to "relax" and you could coax the reading to go down a bit, but eventually, your little stress meter is going to start complaining again. The next step to taking control of the stress in your life is to learn to start respecting your body's stress alerts.

For a few days, devote a small journal to observing and recording your stress levels. For the first 3 or 4 days, try merely putting a number on the stress you feel. You could also just do what seems natural to you – you may choose to use a scale from one to ten, you may choose to map your change in stress with colors, or a diagram of a thermometer slowly rising. If you're feeling creative, you can also choose a symbol or picture to represent your stress levels.

Take a "stress reading" whenever you can manage, throughout the day. Do it first thing when you wake up and just before you go to bed. When you move from one activity or event to another, take a moment to note your stress levels and jot them down. After meals, after particular conversations or at specific times of day, you may notice patterns emerging. Resist the urge to make anything of these patterns for now, simply take faithful recordings and be curious about how you are experiencing stress as the day progresses.

Once you have a few days worth of data, start to add to this by taking fewer, but more detailed "readings". As much as you can, try to identify the *thought* that preceded the moment you took your reading. For example, you take a reading at 16:00 and rate your stress as 5/10. You're thinking, "There's never any time for anything." You note this down. Your kids come home at 16:35, and you take another reading, this one rating stress at 8/10. Your thought immediately preceding is "There's no way I can ever keep up with this." Your last reading for the day is after dinner, at 18:50, with stress at a full 10/10 and the thought, "I have failed, again."

For now, this is just data. Try not to judge the thoughts you put down, and try not to think about any of it too closely. What's important is that you are honest – there is no "right" way to do it. It's also important that your thought statements are as accurate as possible. To identify an accurate thought statement, choose a thought that you feel a strong emotional attachment to. "I'm stressed" is often implied, but try to be more detailed. What does stress mean, in that particular moment? Your underlying emotion may be one of anger, hopelessness or cynicism. Try to nail down this emotion in a thought, and write it down.

What's the point of doing all this? Well, as we've seen, "stress" is a simple word used to describe a very complicated phenomenon. What is stressful for one could be exciting and motivating for another. Nobody experiences the world quite the same way as you do. And it's no use to try and tackle a problem that you don't have a clear understanding of.

By taking a few "stress readings" of our unique responses, we can get a better grasp of what thoughts are operating underneath our physical and emotional reactions. Our emotions, our bodies and our thoughts are all connected, and a change in one produces a change in the other. By identifying our thoughts, we also make the first step in changing them.

You may discover, after a few weeks of listening to what stress is telling you, that there seem to be some themes. In the above example, it may come up again and again that stress is tied to feelings of low self worth. The thoughts may go something along the lines of, "I am no good and I can't deal with all the things I have to do every day. Eventually, I'm going to mess up, and it's going to turn out bad when I do."

The underlying emotion here is one of shame and doubt. Such a person could look at all the things "causing" the stress and try to fix them: send the kids to daycare, take sedative medication, and choose to tell themselves over and over again to "just relax." But none of this will have much effect if they don't address the root of the problem: the thoughts and the emotions attached to them. Until the problem of low self worth is also addressed, stress will keep popping up like a weed.

So, you've gathered some information about yourself and how your mind and heart work. The next step to getting a handle on stress is to accept responsibility for the thoughts that are maintaining that stress. Sure, there may be forces out there in the world that you cannot control, but becoming a strong and resilient person requires you to own your part in perpetuating stress in your life. To change the thoughts you have identified takes courage and a willingness to do something different. If a particular thought has been with you for a long time, it will be hard at first to moderate it. But try anyway.

Your goal in this next exercise is not to identify things or people out in the world who are stressing you. It's to identify your unique response to those things and people. Often with people who are battling stress in their lives, the thoughts they have are not always accurate or healthful. The thought, "I am a failure and I'll never be able to cope" is simply not true. But when you accept it as true, it becomes the source of your stress.

At the end of a few weeks of recording data in this way, you should have a fair idea of the main thought statements that accompany stress in your life. You will start to see recurrent themes. Look at some of the following underlying thoughts and see if you can identify yourself in any of them. These are pretty common themes, but you may have thoughts and feelings very different from these.

- This is not the way the world ought to be (feeling indignant, rage, irritability)

- I have to do X to be loved or to be happy (fear and panic, low self worth)

- Nothing ever works out for me (sadness, hopelessness)

- If I don't do X, something bad will happen (guilt, worry, suspicion)

Your statements may differ, but thoughts of this kind can be recognized easily: they use words like "have to", "should" and "must", or other strong and absolute terms like "never" and "always". Look for statements in the form of conditionals ("If, then" statements) or ones that sound like rules. Statements that talk about "everything" or "nothing" are often thought statements that produce stress, as are statements about "everybody" and "nobody."

Once you have identified your key stress thoughts, write them down again. You may have one or two or a whole handful. We'll be using these statements in the next chapter, where we'll look at ways to start reworking them, unraveling stress from the root up.

Chapter 5: The Behavioral Level: The Power of Habit

Technique One: Challenging

The four example stress statements above are bound to lead to stress. When you fight with reality, the result is always stress and depression. But stressful thoughts only have power over us if we believe in them. If you told a child every day of his life that he was stupid, he'd likely believe it after a while. You are no different. You start to take the things you tell yourself often as absolute gospel. Or to quote Ralph Waldo Emerson: "We become what we think about all day long".

Instead, get into the habit of challenging yourself. Now that you have identified the thoughts that are holding the entire stress response together, have your ears pricked for when you notice those thoughts coming up. And when they do, be ready with a counter-thought. You don't even have to believe it at first, but argue with yourself anyway. For example, if your thought is "I can't do this", counter it with a more balanced, moderate thought. For example, when you catch yourself thinking this, immediately tell yourself, "This is difficult, but I will manage."

The goal is not to go into denial or tell yourself ridiculous stories. Merely moderating the statement is all you need – but make it realistic. So, instead of, "Life sucks", your thought could be, "Life is certainly a challenge!" or even *Today*, life sucks." Change "always" statements to "sometimes". Ask, is your statement strictly true? There may be the odd time when it is true – but the point is to start getting used to double checking these thoughts that you have become accustomed to assuming are true.

This may seem facile on its surface – how could telling yourself a story change how much life sucks that day? The thing is, in time, your brain will begin to believe you. You will get into the habit of challenging yourself, refusing to accept statements that are overly negative and anxious. Remember, life is all about perception.

Technique Two: Do an Accounting

You may know the feeling: your brain keeps on returning to the same image, the same idea. You wake up with it already in your head. You try not to stress about it, but before you know it, your head is going like a hamster in a wheel again. For some, it may work to distract themselves, to think of "nothing", but an anxious person's mind needs to do *something*. Always something.

Instead, sit down with a piece of paper, and draw three columns. The first column should be labeled, "Things I can control", the second column, "Things I can control to some extent" and the third column, "Things I can't control."

Now, take whatever is in your head and dump it out onto the paper. Be honest and realistic. Pretend you are a little computer sorting through every thought and feeling in your head, one by one. What is stressing you out? You may have the thought, "I'm sick of trying to keep up with the housework." You spend time each day cleaning up yet feel your surroundings are always dirty. The more you clean, the more you need to clean. You want to scream and run away, maybe live in a hole in the ground you're so fed up.

Which column can you put "Too much housework" under? This will depend on your unique situation. If it's not your house and you're only staying there temporarily, put it in the last column. If you can afford a cleaner to help once or twice a week, put it in the first. If it's somewhere in between, put it in the middle column.

Be careful though, and watch your bias. Let's say you have an item, "My wife doesn't love me anymore". Where should it go? First of all, this item could be phrased better. You probably don't know this for sure (if you do, well, into the last column it goes). You cannot change how somebody else feels about you, although you can change what *you* feel about *them*. A better way to state it would be, "I am in a marriage where I don't feel loved." This can fit into either of the first two columns. When the problem is framed this way, you are open to realistic solutions. You could leave your marriage, you could seek counseling, you could do any number of things to improve the marriage or your perception of it.

Once you've gotten everything you can think of down on paper, have a good look at it. Take the last column: are there any items here that, if rephrased, can be put into other columns? Remember you are not bending reality, just reframing things. Be curious. "My dog died" certainly belongs in the last column. You can't do a thing about a dead dog. But, if reworded, the statement can also become, "I am grieving for my dog", which could go in the second column. There are many different ways to grieve, and you absolutely have *some* control over how you choose to do it.

Some things we really can't do much about, and that's to be expected. Cancer, losing a job, being born in a particular country, spilling that milk – leave these in the last column. Include here other people's opinions and behavior. You can change your response to them, but if someone doesn't love you, for instance, that's the end of it. If someone has behaved badly toward you, if you've suffered an accident or you're worried about what the weather will be like tomorrow, there's not much you can do about it. It goes in the third column.

Next: tear this column off the rest of the page. If you have a flair for the dramatic, burn it, throw it away or do whatever you need to tell yourself – *this can't be changed.* If it can't be changed, you only damage yourself by stressing about it. Catch yourself thinking about something from the third column? Stop – you already gave it all the thought that's ever going to be necessary.

Now turn to the other two columns. Start with the first column and choose just one item that you have control over. Make just one goal to address this problem. "There is too much housework" can have many possible goals, from hiring outside help, getting family to pull their weight, finding more efficient ways to clean the house, coming to terms with living in filth or moving to a smaller, easier to clean house. If you find yourself stressing about the third column you threw away, come back to the first two columns again and remind yourself: there are things you can change, there are you things you can't. Life is short. Save your energy only for the things you have a realistic chance of changing.

Items in the second column are trickier and can be dealt with once you've handled the more obvious ones. Things like, "People at work don't seem to like me", "I find calculus really hard" and "I'm addicted to heroin" can all be improved, but definitely have some elements that are *somewhat* out of your control. The trick is to slowly start filtering things into the first column. Break knotty items into pieces.

For example, "People at work don't seem to like me" can be separated into, "It's difficult for me to make friends" and "I don't have much in common with my colleagues", for example. The first can definitely be helped, but the second must be put into the last column and accepted – there's no point in stressing over what others have or do not have in common with you. Put your overactive mind to work on the things that have the best chance of changing. Instead of allowing things you can't help to stress you, tune your mind into what can be helped.

Technique Three: Reorient to the Positive

Challenging your thoughts is one thing. But nothing challenges negative thinking as well as cold, hard evidence. If you are fond of telling yourself, "I can't cope with this", try to remember all the times where you, contrary to your belief, actually *did* cope. An anxious mind can gloss over information that doesn't confirm its doom and gloom model of the universe. You may be tempted to say, "Nope, I can't think of anything", but try to cast your mind back to a time when you didn't stress about what you're stressing about now.

Don't get pessimistic about it – *everyone* has had a moment of bliss and peacefulness, a moment when they felt happy and safe and loved, maybe bursting with creativity, maybe immersed in their environment, deep in the flow of things. Put yourself back in that position. Remember it. Ask your mind to acknowledge: there were times when life was different.

It can be hard to envision a future that is better than the present, especially when we are struggling. It's much easier to look to the past and realize that things *do* change, that somewhere, somehow, you knew how to live without stress. Somewhere along the line, you didn't have the problem you have now. When we open our minds up to different possibilities, when we accept that we are living only one possible way out of many ways to live, we become receptive to solutions that we may not have perceived in our stressed out rut.

If you like, try making a list of all your achievements and make a habit of reading through them, to keep a healthy perspective. Take clues from how you have coped with stress in the past.

For example, if you remember that physical activity has helped in the past, see how you can incorporate more physical activity in your life, now.

Technique Four: Learn to Metabolize Negative Feelings

The difference between resilient people and people who crumble under stress is not the amount of stress they experience, but the way they respond to stress when it happens. When you begin to think of stress and adversity as something that is inevitable, even something to embrace, you strengthen yourself against it. You realize quickly what problems are "third column problems" and just get over it.

Rather than forcing yourself to be relentlessly optimistic all the time, simply let your thoughts come. Accept them. Ask yourself, what's the worst that could happen? "My wife could leave me." Ok, really let that settle in. You'd lose your wife, you'd be devastated. And so? People get divorced and go on to live happy and successful lives every day. In fact, for some people, divorce is the best thing that's ever happened to them.

Is it the end of the world? It's tough, sure, but is it *that* terrible? Worriers are prone to catastrophizing and imagining the worst possible outcome. So, indulge yourself. Don't be afraid of the negative emotion your stress is covering. Follow things through to their natural, most disastrous conclusion. Maybe you're worried about messing up your oral presentation, losing your job and becoming the laughing stock of your company. Maybe, it gets as bad as it could possibly get. *So what?* You become a laughing stock, life goes on, you go on.

When we learn to dwell with negative emotions, to endure shame and doubt and rejection and anger, they lose some of their power over us. Many people – in fact some of the world's most successful people – started their success stories only after everything else completely fell to pieces. Human resilience is a real marvel. Yes, your entire life may end today, the things you are worried about may actually happen, and they may be absolutely terrifying. But again, so what? On the other side of disaster, life goes on. A sense of humor will help more than any empty positive thinking platitude.

Chapter 6: The Relational and Spiritual Level: Anxiety Free Dating and Relationships

The previous section looked at some possible ways to counter and reframe "stress thoughts", so that we can transform our nervous and anxious energy to a more realistic way of tackling our problems. You may be tempted to skip this section if you are already in a happy relationship or aren't concerned with dating at this moment. But keep reading - "dating" may seem like a very specific area to focus our attention on, but actually, the way we interact with others is a key part of the topic of stress and learning to live with less of it.

To put it simply, our relationships with others are reflections of our relationship with ourselves and with the world in general. Nowhere is it more obvious how a change in mindset can change the entire tone of our living, than with dating and relationships. When we encounter others, we make ourselves vulnerable, we put our self esteem to the test, we take a risk and trust someone else with our hearts and minds. If you are one of those people tormented by your lack of "social skills", insecurity or jealousy, then a look at the role that stressful thinking plays in your relationships may be helpful.

Learning to Trust

When we first come into the world, we are naive and completely trusting. We are the most vulnerable, physically and psychologically, that we will ever be. Yet we willingly go into the arms of strangers, waddle into new and possibly dangerous situations and put any old thing into our mouths. Somewhere along the line, we develop more caution. We realize that not everything is to be trusted, and we narrow our range, trusting only those that earn that trust.

At the root of much anxiety and worry is a lack of trust. Anxiety is future oriented and its core premise is that in the future, someone or something may harm you. The response is to be vigilant, to try to prevent that harm from happening. Whether we lack trust in other people, in the world around us or even in ourselves, this orientation is simply exhausting.

Lack of Trust in Others

Fear of rejection, shyness and being withdrawn are the result of looking at the possibility of interaction with others, and overestimating the harm they could possibly bring to you. In other words, it's the absence of trust that people are fundamentally good and will treat you well. This feeling could stem from your family of origin, where you may have been taught that people never tell the truth or will hurt you if given half the chance.

In the dating realm, this manifests as the belief that almost everyone is out to get you, cynicism about the opposite sex and a tendency to interpret every behavior as proof that nobody could ever be trusted to give you what you really need. Sadly, stress that results from this can never be soothed – you have no control over how people treat you, and when you are withdrawn and unwilling to open up, the paradox is that people are less likely to trust *you*.

Lack of Trust in the World

This reflects a bigger picture – that in the world at large, we don't feel safe and cared for. We don't trust that the universe is basically a safe and reasonable place to inhabit. If we believe that most people are not to be trusted as sources of love and support, we can begin to think of the entire world that way. We sigh and succumb to "dog eat dog" laws, we think that if something can go wrong, it will. We become fatalistic in our interactions with others. We see the opposite sex as nothing more than extensions of this unfriendly world, ready to inflict more damage onto us. In other words, intimacy is something that needs to be defended against. Whether you've decided to shun people all together and live as a "self-sufficient" hermit, or whether you've latched onto hate for another group as the source of all your difficulties, a mistrustful attitude to the world hurts *you* the most.

Lack of Trust in Ourselves

Self confidence is trust in your own abilities. It is a feeling of being safe in your own competence as a human being. You may not know what the future holds, but a strong self esteem assures you that you act from you principles, and will probably be OK. Lacking trust in ourselves leads to insecurity. It is the doubt that we have any power over how our lives pan out. It is the disbelief in our own competence, our own goodness, and our own process. We may defer judgment to others simply because we don't believe we can be trusted to make good decisions ourselves. We may become dependent, choosing to forfeit our agency and believe that in general, we are helpless and hopeless.

We can see that with Mike, the man we met earlier, the details of his wife's possible infidelity are only one side of the story. Mike may have, on closer inspection, a problem with trust in general. He can't surrender to the idea that his wife will not harm him, he can't believe that the world is not hostile, not unfriendly, and worst of all, he doesn't trust that he himself is lovable enough to win his wife's continued affection. What removes Mike from him wife is not her infidelity, but Mike's own thoughts and beliefs.

On the surface, what looks like a fairly superficial first date, or a "lover's quarrel", for instance, can actually press deep anxiety buttons within us, can bring out our most fundamental beliefs about ourselves and the world, and get directly to the heart of the way we are oriented to the outside world. Relationships are stressful!

But if we put our guard up, we deny ourselves the opportunity to connect deeply with others. If we are unwilling to open up and accept the risk of pain, we are left with empty or hollow connections that don't truly satisfy us. We are unable and unwilling to metabolize negative feelings. If we lack a basic trust in ourselves, the situation is worse – we don't believe we can hold onto love even when we have it; we become jealous, dependent, suspicious.

On a deeper spiritual level, Mike is fixed in this position of mistrust. From this, the thought "she is probably cheating on me" goes unchallenged. The longer it is held onto, the more it is assumed to be truth. The idea that his wife would leave is unthinkable, and causes him great pain. These thoughts and emotions affect his physical body as much as if he had actually been attacked in the alley that night. The stress trickles down and affects each and every area of his being.

In reality, even if his wife were to leave, it may be the case that this is a good outcome, and one that he actually needs. But he is unwilling to accept and manage this "negative" emotion. He chooses not to listen to what his anxiety is telling him. He incorrectly assumes the source of his trouble is his wife, when in fact his thoughts about his wife are to blame. He tries to control her, but nothing she can do will ease his suspicions. He tries to dull his stress with substances. He forces himself to ignore it. At this point, whether his wife is or is not unfaithful is scarcely the point. What is problematic is that Mike lacks trust in himself, in others and in the world he lives in. In the bigger picture, he doesn't trust the process he is in.

Chapter 7: Your Personal Stress Map

At its most basic, stress removes us from reality. Stress is future oriented, and forces our minds to live in places of "what if" rather than an appreciation for what is, right now, in the moment. In some cases, stress is just the thing we need to kick us into gear and meet that deadline, stand up for ourselves or leave a situation that isn't working. Stress is a biological and psychological phenomenon, but it also entails a deeper, even spiritual dimension. For most people today, stress is a complicated interplay of body, mind and soul.

Stress is not something that can be fixed with tips, tricks and hacks. It is a problem with our perception of reality; it is a mistake in appraisal of the universe around us. Stress can be (temporarily) eased by managing the purely biological or cognitive dimension. But stress is, at the deepest level, a philosophical orientation and a way of thinking about the world.

To ease stress in our lives, we need to approach every aspect of the problem.

You may take a long, honest look at your life and begin to identify what is really going on, and what is really at the heart of this deceptively simple problem we call "stress". Here's an example of a "stress map" that may emerge as you start to incorporate some of these techniques and ideas into your life. This one is for the hypothetical Mike:

Physically:

Mike realizes his caffeine addiction is propping him up and damaging his cortisol levels. He quits coffee and takes up a daily breathing exercise to ensure that he is breathing deeply and slowly, something he usually forgets about when caught up in his thoughts. He chooses to actively notice when he's clenching his teeth or tightening his muscles and makes a point of having "time out" sessions to remember his breath and become mindful again.

Emotionally:

He notices how strongly tied his physical reactions are to his emotional states. Behind a lot of his suspicion and fearfulness is the underlying feeling of being small and ineffectual. He constantly feels under threat. In time, he understands this stems from being raised by parents who were inconsistent with their affection. He feels as though sooner or later, people are going to realize how terrible he is, and stop loving him. He tries to notice when he worries about rejection and actively chooses to let it go. He is stressed because he is constantly processing the thought: "I am inferior". To combat this, he takes up martial arts and cultivates an attitude of competence and mastery over himself.

Cognitively:

To help him deal with these feelings he has, he realizes he has developed thoughts to explain this shame to himself. He tells himself, over and over and over again, "I need to be vigilant, I need to keep up or I will be a failure, I need to win people's love and be on the look out for any sign that they are going to withdraw it". These are repeated so often that the brain starts to perceive them as truth. Instead, he teaches himself to challenge these thoughts when they pop up. The more rational perspective is that he cannot change other people's behavior, only his own. He turns his attention away from stewing over his wife, and creates more opportunities for himself that prove that he is basically a good and lovable person.

Relationally:

He craves, almost more than anything, the love and acceptance of women, but at the same time he's keenly aware that they are just another thing on the list to be managed, another source of rejection. He distrusts most women, and when this shuts him out of meaningful connections with them, he takes this as evidence that they couldn't be trusted. And so his feelings of isolation deepen. With his wife, he cannot believe that she truly loves him – how could anyone love him? She must be lying. Here, Mike makes more of an effort to befriend women in casual settings.

Spiritually:

It feels as though it's him against the world. He's apathetic, anxious and mistrustful. Deep down, he believes the world is fundamentally hostile. He doesn't have the feeling that life can be left alone to carry on. So, he stresses about it. What's the meaning of it all? He grows cynical and has no faith that he is a part of something bigger, something that he can relax inside of. He starts keeping a journal and becomes reacquainted with his desire for a simpler, humbler life. He finds spiritual comfort in his martial arts practice, a minimalistic lifestyle, and begins to let in the thought that he has a purpose in life, and can surrender to the unknown and the mystery of his fate.

Mike will not be successful in reducing stress levels by taking medication (a physical solution) or consulting a psychologist to get to the root of his self-defeating thoughts (a cognitive solution) or arranging a romantic getaway with his wife (a relational solution). He could go to church or burn sage and meditate, but it will mean nothing if every other area is business as usual. His solution has to be comprehensive, and address each level.

What is *your* personal stress map? On each of these axes, where are you now? A solution will acknowledge all of these areas, and the best solutions will link into one another. The person feeling overwhelmed with work could decide to exercise more, which will give her more confidence which will affect her sense of trust in herself. Exercising could combat the persistent thought "I can't cope with anything" - evidence of a completed marathon will definitely shift this belief.

A firmer sense of self esteem translates to healthier boundaries and expectations with other people: she may decide she is strong enough to let her guard down, and when she does, she is pleasantly surprised to learn: other people are not the cause of her stress. Perhaps the world is not such a dark and hostile place as she thought? Instead of neurotically stewing over what could possibly happen in the future, she becomes an active agent who has faith in her ability to change it. What to do about the excess housework will flow naturally from this understanding.

Chapter 8: The Blessings of Negative Thinking

Our positive thinking, self-help obsessed society treats stress as the common cold of the psychological world – something that everyone has, something that nobody wants. We are encouraged to do whatever we can to get rid of it. This attitude, however, is seldom productive. Stress is not merely something that sits on top of our lives and merely needs to be taken off to reveal the tranquility underneath. Stress is a *part* of us, and indicates that something, somewhere is wrong.

Stress is a blessing in disguise that alerts us to exactly the areas that need our attention. Insomnia is not a disease that deserves a heavy sleeping tablet or alcohol, but rather proof that even if we don't understand it at the moment, our minds and spirits are working hard at fixing whatever is out of whack.

Successful people who live stress free may disappoint others who look closely at what their lives actually entail: they have exactly the same amount of stress and adversity as everyone else. They may do nothing special. But underneath is a radically different way of perceiving themselves and their worlds. If you have sought out this book and read this far, it means your instinct for growth and well-being is intact.

Congratulations!

Now, what are you going to do about it?

Chapter 9: Living Stress-Free: Moving Forward

Once you're equipped with a deeper appreciation of *why* you stress, you're in the best position to move forward in your task of reducing stress in your life – forever. As we've seen, the multifaceted nature of stress means it needs a multifaceted solution. While meditation, supplements or a visit to a life-coach are all valuable, they are not always enough to combat stress on their own.

Instead, stress needs to be respected as the warning flag it is, and an approach that acknowledges your body, your mind, your heart and soul is going to be much more lasting and effective than a Band-Aid solution like sedative medication or "productivity hacks".

Fortunately/unfortunately, you are the only one who can truly make changes in the way you experience your life. So much of what is aimed at stress reduction fails, even if it's good advice, because people are afraid or unwilling to face up to the challenges that are keeping them locked in a cage of anxiety, self-doubt and stress.

Stress can leave us feeling helpless in a chaotic and unfriendly world. The antidote is learning to trust yourself again, and gradually taking the risks to make changes in your daily habits and the way you interact with other people. Anxiety is about a loss of control, a loss of faith and a rupture in the connection between us and others.

If you have found anything that resonates with you in this book, challenge yourself to make some changes – *now*. Not tomorrow or at some ill-defined point in the future. Become curious about yourself as you construct your own personalized "stress map" and begin keeping a journal of your thoughts. Be receptive to change and trust that you have it in you to become more relaxed, more confident and surer of your day-to-day life.

Such a stress-free person is able to face adversity head on, and knows in their heart of hearts that they will never be ruffled for long. A person who is in control of their lives is not damaged or frightened by stress, and even when it arises, they are able to engage with it and even be thankful for the lessons it can teach them about how to be better. In other words, they are robust and resilient because their sense of faith in themselves allows them to approach the world openly, with curiosity instead of fear.

Have faith that in time, you can become that person.

Finally, I would love to hear how this book has helped you, so if you liked this book I would really appreciate it if you'd leave a review and tell me all about it. You can leave a review by searching for the title of this book on www.amazon.com.

Bonus: Preview of "Minimalism: How To Declutter, De-stress and Simplify Your Life With Simple Living"

Today, a growing number of people are becoming dissatisfied with their lives and turning to simpler ways of working, living and raising their children. This book will explore the philosophy of minimalism and how it can streamline your life, declutter your home, reduce stress and reconnect you to what's truly important.

You'll find ways to adopt a mindset that promotes simplicity and elegance in your every day life, and rethink your dependence on material possessions. Whether in our wardrobes, kitchens, work lives or our deeper sense of personal and spiritual purpose, we could all do with focusing on things that align with our values and reducing the distraction of those things that pull us away from them. This book shows you how.

For those born and raised in the height of our consumer society, the idea that happiness and personal fulfillment is found in *stuff* is more or less a given. The capitalist machine we all live within requires only one thing of us: that we should constantly want, and the things we should want are to be found, usually, in malls. Malls that are filled with strategically placed advertising, with the sole purpose to entice and lure you, trying to convince you that you need, not want, their specific product. Our economy relies heavily on a steady stream of consumption: better clothes, cars, bigger houses and things to fill those houses with, the newest appliances, Christmas decorations, pet toys, jewelry, office furniture, pot plants, gaming consoles, specialty tires, luxury soaps... the array of stuff is simply dazzling.

But if you are reading this there's a chance you find this overabundance just a little... exhausting. Paradoxically, there seems to be a sad sort of emptiness in filling up one's life with more things. What is simple and truly valuable often seems to be completely hidden under mountains of what is unnecessary. Although advertising tells us the best way to solve problems is to *buy* solutions, tranquility and a graceful life seem to elude us, no matter what we buy or how much of it.

Minimalism is an aesthetic, a philosophy and a way of life. This book takes a look at how deeply liberating a simpler life can be, and shows you ways you can adopt a calmer, more deliberate way of living and working. Minimalism is about clearing away the clutter that is distracting from what is really important. It's about rethinking our attitudes to ownership, to our lifestyles and to our innermost values.

This book will give practical advice on owning fewer clothes, de-cluttering your life, simplifying your daily routine and reducing mindless consumerism. It will also explore how practical changes to our surroundings can lead to a previously unknown inner peace and calm.

Other Books By This Author

- Minimalism: How To Declutter, De-Stress And Simplify Your Life With Simple Living

- The Minimalist Budget: A Practical Guide On How To Save Money, Spend Less And Live More With A Minimalist Lifestyle

- Mindful Eating: A Healthy, Balanced and Compassionate Way To Stop Overeating, How To Lose Weight and Get a Real Taste of Life by Eating Mindfully

- Self-Esteem For Kids - Every Parent's Greatest Gift: How To Raise Kids To Have Confidence In Themselves And Their Own Abilities

Made in the USA
Lexington, KY
27 October 2017